Being

Full of Light,

Insubstantial

To Eileen,
The most substantial
light in my life!

Linda D. Addison

7/28/07

Being

Full of Light,

Insubstantial

Original Photography and Variations
by Brian James Addison

SPACE AND TIME
New York

Original photograph and variations by Brian James Addison
Book design by Terry Bradshaw

Space and Time
138 West 70th Street
New York, New York 10023-4468

CONTENTS

un

ing

Acknowledgments

Grateful recognition to the editors and publishers of the publications in which some of the poems in this collection originally appeared, as follows:

"The Barn" ©2000 by *The Edge*

"Turning" ©2001 by *Rough Beasts,* Lone Wolf Publications

"Night Visitors Made Flesh, In The Vessel of Your Creativity" ©2001 by *GSHW In A Fearful Way*

"Burning in the Shadows, While My Pen Softly Bleeds" ©2001 by *GSHW In A Fearful Way*

"After The Fire" ©2002 by *Dark Voices: A Collection of Poetry from the Writers of Wicked Verse,* Flesh & Blood Press

"Dreams of the Night Bird" ©2002 by *Dark Voices: A Collection of Poetry from the Writers of Wicked Verse,* Flesh & Blood Press

"The Cosmic Adventures of Jar Boy" ©2002 by *African Voices*

"Cookin Now" ©2003 by *Flesh & Blood*

"Evolving" ©2003 by *Strange Horizons*

"Fleeting Light" ©2004 by *Spooks,* Twilight Tales

"After the Tsunami" ©2005 by *SpiderWords.com*

"Between" ©2005 by *SpiderWords.com*

"Dark Dreamers" ©2005 by *Necon25* convention book

"Holding You" ©2005 by *SpiderWords.com*

"How To Wear War" ©2005 by *SpiderWords.com*

"I'll Take My Truth On The Side" ©2005 by *SpiderWords.com*

"Nightshift" ©2005 by *WHC 2005* convention book

"poem #3" ©2005 by *The Dead Cat Poet Cabal* anthology, Bedlam Press

"poem crazy" ©2005 by *WHC 2005* convention book

"Storm of Souls" ©2005 by *Fantastic Stories*

"Wet" ©2005 by *SpiderWords.com*

"Mami Wata, Goddess of Clear Blue" upcoming issue of *Anansi: Fiction of the African Diaspora*

"After the Tsunami", "Between", "Dreams of the Night Bird", "Nightshift", "Storm of Souls", "Wet" are on the Honorable Mention list for various editions of St Martin's Press, *Year's Best Fantasy & Horror.*

Navajo Prayer

I will be happy forever.
Nothing will hinder me.
My words will be beautiful.
Walk in peace brothers and sisters.
I walk with beauty before me.
I walk with beauty behind me.
I walk with beauty above me.
I walk with beauty around me.

becoming

River Share

We share the same soul
   even as our breath moves separately
two billion exhales, inhales
   the River runs beneath our skin
joy, pain, tears, laughter
   runs beneath the River.

Let me breathe in
   your fear
taste your tears,
   the River runs sweet and salty
with endless cycles of the moon
   two billion breaths undulate,
a wave up and down.

Let us share this soil
   even as our breath moves separately
two billion drops in the River
   infinite possibilities, one River
undulates in and out,
   no difference beneath the skin,
your tears taste the same as mine.

nebulae, stars weave
pocket universe
celestial garland

Mami Wata, Goddess of Clear Blue

Worry sings bright in your neurons,
your light so blurred I could barely taste you
    while I was sleeping, dreaming of the time before
    I melted down two galaxies making my way here
    why you wait so long to call for me, baby?

Your pain is clean and clear in the thickening tattoos on your back
    you no longer hunger for us in your dreams
    silence has softened your soul, eaten at your aspect
    you rest in my arms now, it's going to be alright.

I used to visit the voodoo pantheons when you gyrated in dusty courtyards
    back when you came to us free and open in your sleep
    Mami Vishnu and I introduced star maps to the faithful
    crowded your dreams with tomorrows full of luminosity.

Brought your children to my lap, just like you now,
let them look through my eyes
    into the darkness to see nothing is empty
    leaned their heads against my belly
    so they could hear the purr of the Never-Born.

What took you from us is the hard things you build
so you could forget the soft things
    but hunger for a way to live without bruised outstretched hands
    don't just go away because you fill the night with bright lights
    making the moon and stars blush with neglect.

You always hungry for things to fill your hands and pockets,
shiny unneeded things
    I stayed with you because with all that wanting
    you made an opening for me
    couldn't resist your eyes rolled white upward and inward to me
    you know how vain we can be, it's vanity hurting you now, baby.

There's always a way to heal—you got to know where to look
    what matters is the sharp edges behind your closed eyes
    I savored the small wounds unhealed in your heart
    even when my name laid dead in your mouth.

First Day

Dawn
   the first breath
   of a new day
angels
   cross the sky
   bands of new light
humanity
   deprived providence
   stones in the heart
hope
   twirling shadows
   on dusty ground
sun
   across blue
   stretched enclosure
moon
   waiting
   dusk's door.

Dark Dragon

(WHILE IN A PLANE TO WISCONSIN)

No sky peeks through white clouds above
    instead a dark dragon outlined,
tail extended across open expanse
    flying to Milwaukee today,
where are you headed?

Together in the sky, above the clouds
    below in gathering morning light
car lights glow orange, strange lava flow,
    we climb higher, even hidden
I feel your wings above
    as you fly higher
    impossibly higher.

My soul
    clings tightly
    to your scaly back.

Chatoyant Love

(personal)

light then dark
   your love shifts in the evening light,
shining in the dark like cat eyes
   you see into the corners of my desire
shifting my thoughts to only you,
    shining in the light, stunning and bright
you breath into the heart of my dreams
   bringing focus to only you
pushing all doubt to the four corners of tomorrow,
   deep gemstone light, too bright.

(not personal)

light then dark
   love shifts in the evening light,
shining in the dark like cat eyes
   seeing into the corners of desire
shifting thoughts,
    shining in the light, stunning and bright
breathing into the heart of dreams
   bringing focus
pushing all doubt to the four corners of tomorrow,
   deep gemstone light, too bright.

*chatoyant: having a changeable luster, a gleam like a cat's eye

Power Surge

How it goes, life as usual, then
   a surge of heat along the neck, chest
"pay attention", breathing through until coolness
   comes again, how to describe this feeling,
body acting of its own accord, what is the message?

Talking or listening as usual, then
   heat spikes in neck, chest, "change is coming",
irritating thoughts occur, what about what is needed
   all the years of giving, what about receiving,
all the years of compromising, there is a message here.

Waiting for the ancestors' sweet whisper, then
   hot energy flows, fire that doesn't burn
"be authentic", ah-h-h yes, no reason to wait
   this is the time to speak, not just listen,
receive, not just give, the village can wait.

Today is the first day of the rest of life . . .

A New Day

nu-neo-new
   human-hu-woman
wu-man
   neo-wu-man.

River of Silent Dreams

Trees grow on the distant bank
    imagined beaches breath in,
needing to hear water lap gently against
    fallen branches, desire lies deep
under sandy soil, listening to the bloom of
    newborn Dream Trees.

When will sleeping seeds sprout, push
    through rocky soil and wobbly hope,
gentle rain waits patiently
    to rinse away past fears,
ghostly shadows of restraint weaken
    in the bright light of a new day.

Release all breath, break through
    hard outer shell, grow up into rich earth,
let tender new growth crush sadness
    remove clenched wishes reborn
in the invincible shadow of Dream Trees,
    begin anew . . .

Transcending

Being an island in a small frozen
    lake, thinking to fool night
into day, eyes closed, avoiding
    great doubt, wondering
whether committing to do what
    it takes is worth what is wanted.

In the world of humans, driving
    on a path, one foot in front of another,
waiting for a similar effect
    as the dream, bright lights,
animals, small and tall enter
    dancing, wanting nothing
more than to float in the shadows.

Multi-syllables wait at the door
    hoping to define passion
with published manifestations
    reaffirming systematic
autopsies, sometimes the open hand
    is just a hand.

Nightshift

Raven, sweet dark dream
   split open my eyes
peel away my hope, bring me
   your joyless cry, your visions
held tight in a decaying breast.

I drink my desire
   from the sharp folds of your wings
lie naked in your beak, become a seed.

Let me rise in the endless night
   through your dying breath.

Possibilities

I could fly for you
    into the sun
endure melting
    wax, feathers,
dreams.

I could fry for you
    into the fire
survive evaporating
    tears, fear,
desire.

I could phase for you
    into the future
dismiss spinning
    guns, swords,
exhalations.

I could
    you could
      we . . .

The Cosmic Adventures of Jar Boy

Born anonymously he floated in his own miraculous birth waters
    large unblinking eyes, lipless mouth, short flippers for arms and legs
curled in a glass container, making the circus rounds
    until sold to a scientist who wanted to dissect him
but stopped after a long glance into his large eyes and never remembered
    putting him in a shady corner of a sunny inventory room.

There his mind drifted and reached into the dreams of others,
    to run and dance and love, until he didn't care if he was dreaming
or awake in other's minds, night and day blinked through the room's
    one window, no one visited the dusty space
he shared with obsolete computers and broken chairs.

He reached farther and farther on an endless lake of wishes
    he found a dancer who wanted to be a pilot
a pilot who wanted to be President,
    a President who wanted to be an astronaut,
an astronaut who wanted to live forever.

Carried beyond earth's gravity, he marveled at the luminous disk
    that held his jar, skipping once more he touched something vast and alien
and brilliantly hungry, and in it he gave birth to swirling star clusters,
    licked the icy trail of comets, watched life grow—mature—die
on other planets, followed a black hole as it ate its way through a billion galaxies.

Until homesickness made him wonder of his first home and his tiny body
    in its snug jar, so he returned to the third rock from the sun to find
all of the little and big humans turned to dust, his jar buried deep
    under miles of volcanic rock, and he wished he could cry just one last time
before returning to his journey through eternity.

Darklight, Star Bright

(for Tanya Emma)

A nest of angels reside in her eyes,
    unable to turn away you want to see - what she sees,
hungry for visions of past and future dreams
    you open your heart to her smile and let the soft rain
wash away weary thoughts born of the day.

Her limbs long and graceful, her mind sharp and vast,
    in her eyes lies the hope of tomorrow's breath,
in her eyes, sweet dark truth,
    for these times of deception,
her dark light sweeps away those dependent on non-think,
    the way of unraveling begins in her smile.

A nest of angels dwell on her fingertips
    unwilling to turn away you watch exquisite constructs pour
from her moving hands, transform from two dimensions
    to dance into the cosmos. . .you smile, wanting
the soft rain of her creations to wash away not so hidden regret.

Her limbs graceful and long, her mind vast and sharp,
    there is no place to parry, you retreat
wondering if truth is what you really want or
    to continue in the dim shadows of life. . .she surrounds
you with acceptance, Salute, this match is over,
    you surrender to the soft reality of her dark light.

In the nest of angels where life is born, scarlet feathers
    gather, edged in shadows, fearless in their gentle way,
you think of her and remember warm rain
    unraveling the emptiness, the hard walls. . .you smile,
this day is made new in her eyes, as are you.

Back Story

We are the back story
   born and living
in the soap opera made
   from the bones of our ancestors,
smiling, they wait for the moment
   we finally awaken,

the truth:

we are light beings
   flesh
merely a shadow
   breath
a pause between
   birth and death
every moment
   past and future
does not exist,
   now
is actualization,

perceptions
   limit immortality
one bite of the apple
   and the show begins.

Wrong/Right

Wrong twists around tense neck
   supporting training
   years in the making
   coils in the gut
   tiny razors removing history.

Right blooms in day, dreaming
   unlimited by sex, race, politics
   boundaries dissipate
   day by day, moment by moment
   growing in ripe flesh soil.

Being in the middle
   of a vision
   measurements vanish,
   own the exhalation
   inhalation, heart beat,
   point the finger inside.

Evolving

Freezing rain clicks on the bus window
    water, the first liquid
the place of beginning life
    returning, ever returning
to this place, four wheels, an engine
    one driver, many riders
jerking down a pathway to eternity.

Moonlight reflects off wet sidewalks
    the world made new
by past tears, primordial mist
    revealed in spots of soft light
our intrusion to evolution
    metal, plastic, glass
running down a roadway to infinity.

Riding through my place in time
    living in the movie of Earth
"Cut!" this scene is done
    tears of the dinosaurs
clicking on window panes
    I remember mud, warm and sweet
my flippers sliding in gritty reality.

Whispering in my genes, our genes
    all yesterdays barely hiding
in my mouth, lips pressed close
    the synchronicity of one breath
I taste eternity on the fingertips
    of this day, where the secrets
beat in the heart, the freezing rain.

Dream Walking

Walking in a dream
   steps on the Path,
fog surrounding days
   full throttle movement outside
forcing reason
   outside
alienness such as this,

living without thought
   breathing on the Path
raw on the edge of a day
   empty movement inside
being a dream
   inside
aspects such as this,

being alien in a dream
   the Path blooming inside
full without thinking
   between breaths, another
aspect moves inside
   outside
such here-ness as this.

Cleaning List

Sweep floors
   Gather old dreams
Do laundry
   Bring in fresh desire
Buy milk and juice
   Fold up joy
Pick up children from school
   Drop off envy
Press shirts
   Hang up anger
Buy new shoes
   Freeze greed
Wash windows
   Laugh loudly
Dust tables
   Make love.

Interruption

In my mouth
　　Lies wait quietly
to advise the Dreams.

I close my lips tightly
　　afraid of loss
my eyes look to the horizon
　　searching for decaying stars.

I see shards of yesterday
　　glittering in the air
not falling up or down
　　there is a pattern.

The almost words spell out
　　unwise advice,
jumbled phone numbers
　　names of my enemies.

The whine of dry laughter
　　dances under my feet,
uneven, jagged, bitter sweet
　　I don't want to fall
where is the handhold?

How to reach within
　　find the key, unlock the Dreams
forgive the madness?

The Adventures of a Ghetto Child in the Universe

Voice stilled and distant, hands empty
   looking up at a clear night sky, where is hope
where is the light to pull thorns of hunger
   from tender skin, stars sparkle above,
how close are they?

Hatched from a neglected life, looking up
   stars beckon, gravity frees
thin arms and legs, looking up hunger drifts away
   stars bright, wink and open up, fitting one child
into their infinite embrace.

Questions drift away, leaving misty trails in the night sky
   having traveled no where, now into a universe
vast and unbounded, time stops, space unfolds,
   one child's atoms spread out, remade into
clouds: round, angular, long, short, wild, happy.

There is no hunger in the place of no time,
   expansive shadows float below, cloud shapes
make shadow puppets on a sleeping world,
   letting go, reaching up and out, eyes close,
one child, waiting to be seen, enters a universe.

Being life, unfolding, bright light in dark sky
   one child sees everything, becomes everything
there is no difference between
   this and that, yesterday and tomorrow,
a child smiles, finding a place in wild stars.

One

Given one word, kiss it gently
   lay it down, kicking and glittery
in this place, a sun rises, voices chant,
   bones awaken, old and new,
to dance and sing.

This place, beyond past and future, where
   fearless voices chant, ground
covered in golden wheat, air crisp and sweet
   one sound, carried in the wind
wakens those who hunger for more.

This healing, becoming One,
   pours divine order into the Universe
delivering power to love
   breaking old patterns of pain
filling hunger, one is greater than two.

Surrender one gentle light,
   lie down in this place,
allow sunrises in your heart
   listen to earthsong, chants
of ancestors waking to forgive.

Never forget the one promise
   infinite, expansive Light
one can redeem all
   one creates healing,
awakens new magic.

Mp3 Zen Buddhists

Meditation for the 21st Century
    easily done, empty minds no challenge,
music pours in, suppressing doubt, anger,
    frustration, thoughts of bills and disappointment,
music pounding through white, black ear phones
    rocking the moment, dismissing erratic past,
unreliable futures,

staying in the Now, easily done,
    state of no-mind completed
by the flick a switch, music filling
    spaces between, erasing time,
delivering bodies as they travel from
    here to there, without thought.

Mp3 Zen Buddhists fill the streets, urban,
    suburban homes and stores,
having arrived in the no-place, at the root
    of their being, surrounded with their own
sound tracks, what is the way of nature
    when earphones easily deliver no-thought.

Useless Things

Why do I need to do these things
   useless as they seem, no money, no time is given
stolen moments as receipts, rejections pile in dusty corners,
   no time to clean, just spin words out of blood,
hungry for completion,
   characters and images possess my day and night.

I want to relax, watch useless entertainment,
   not feel the endless pressure,
words spinning wildly in my soul,
   my eyes look at the horizon,
pulled in other-where, other-time, I leave here,
   enter worlds hungry to be born, sit for hours, typing,
ignoring relentless chores.

Trying to stop, once I held my breath for three years,
   hungry dreams lingered in shadowy closets
until bursting through,
   my life exploded with change,
I let everything out,
   I am a day dreamer.

I continue to dream,
   allow strange song to sting
through my eager hands.

I must breathe.

poem crazy

Let's go crazy
    let's make elephant soufflé
twirl Mars and Venus on the ends
    of our dreams, make love
in the shadows of black holes
    weave the echoes of nightmares
into a mask of all-time
    sweat until our wounds heal
in a tent spun from the smooth
    sweet skin of unborn devotion
let's write a poem.

(In Our Bodies Lie) The History of No End

In the   space   between   day and night
    you hear muddy birth waters
first
    life
        u n d u l a t i n g
            from no place
        into some place
carrying more >> than imagination
    beyond
what flows from lips   hidden   repressed   delivered

Your body sings
    of the beginning
before
    time
        was born
listen
    to the speck of. . .star dust
nestled (in) enduring bones

pragmatic lines and curves   holding   nurturing   sustaining

    binding you to its ancestors
the first matter
    elusive dark energy
        forces of incredible devotion

waiting
    patiently waiting
to begin
    a dazzling dance

your atoms echo   the first birth
    movement brought forth by
the breath of an awakening
    the opening
an infinite point in begin-time

releasing
     galaxies   planets   suns   moons

flesh shaped to capture

   mouths watering for
   hearts yearning for
   hands pleading for
creations yet seen
   empty expanse unanswered
      visions crying to be unborn

Do not fear
   what can not   end
you
   are
      cut from the fabric
   of infinite unfolding
all that is
   ever was
      ever will be

The heartbeat
   of those   yet to come
sleep
   in the shadows
      of your genes.

Imagine

Transforming
    what was once a season of dreams
into winters for the stars
    there can be dragons
ashes, brimstone, green diamond
    scales dissolving in morning light.

Let us become mythical creatures
    give birth to multi-verses
shaping time and space into origami
    light to devour wasted moments,
cycle around and around old visions,
    make new songs and stories.

un

Ghost Dancing with the White Buffalo

I, the shadow,
        large head, thick shoulders, strong legs,
        drawn to the light,
        dirt under fingernails,
        Mother Earth – giver of life,
        we dance to your love,

        hi-ya, hi-ya,

        accept our worn souls,
        let our dance become part of
        your promise to the People,

        hi-ya, hi-ya,

        our children's unborn voices
        cry for the morning light,
        the world has lost its heart,

        hi-ya, hi-ya,

        forgive our arrogance,
        our closed eyes,
        let love lead us back
        to compassion,

        hi-ya, hi-ya.

As the Dust Settles

(09-11-01)

The stars cry
   500 feet above
   the darkening crater,
   wound in the soul of a city, a nation,

   1000 feet above
   the spot of flatness
   where two buildings once stood,

   5000 feet above
   a dot in the heart of Earth
   surrounded by points of light.

The stars cry
   listening to the ripple of sound
   still reverberating in open space
   waves moving to universe's edge,

   in the ribbon of existence
   where time and space play
   inevitable cruelty casts another bloody shadow.

Wilderness of Mirrors

In the wilderness of mirrors
    lies become truth
homely reverts to beauty
    all dreams invert
to nightmares.

In the wilderness of mirrors
    no one says anything
meaning everything
    no desire is fulfilled
loss inverts into money.

Wandering from reflection
    to reflection, alternate egos
meet themselves, seeking
    recognition in the
wilderness of mirrors.

Hungry for redemption
    new creatures try
to smile at the dying stares
    waiting in the shiny
surfaces untouched by guilt.

Turn away from the false
    likeness, wash hands
clean, follow the true setting
    sun, not its reflection in the
wilderness of mirrors.

ego
    sharp teeth
    infinite hunger
nails scratching
    on a blackboard.

How to Wear War

Never sleep or drink beer,
    tread lightly on razor sharp nightmares
thrown at your feet,
    look at the stranger in the mirror
looking back at you.

Talk to your '93 Chevy
    but not your spouse,
blame surviving on dumb luck,
    cry when everyone laughs
laugh when others sleep.

Release another's throat
    if found in your grip,
paint your scars neon orange,
    never look at the sun,
swallow food without chewing.

Avoid shadows—only you can
    see the blood there.

Never speak while the sun sets
    or rises,
leave your body
    when a loud sound happens.

Sleep on the floor,
    make a collage from the Percocet,
Elavil, Vicodin, Benadryl they give you,
    have a map of the United States
tattooed on your back in invisible ink.

Wet

(for TT)

Hungry to taste you, I reach inside
    myself for reasons to desire
no one else, my soul is wet, my nails
    sharp, your words fill me with
Shadows.

Hungry to be you, I reach inside
    wet pain sears my eyes
burning my tongue, your words taste me
    erasing my soul, filling me with
Shadows.

Time has no arms to hold me,
    wet pain removes my eyes
my soul burns with reason,
    no words find me, I am filled with
Shadows.

Secret Places

There are wolves at the door
    don't look at the light in their eyes
    they only want to lick your sweetness
    harm is not in their hearts, they are only animals
    what could they be thinking.

There are dreams in the trash
    don't look at the dying light in their souls
    they only want to live in your eyes
    lick the tears from your denial, they are not real
    what could they be thinking.

There are nasty things in the shadows
    don't look at their outline in open hands
    they only want to tear at your mouth
    remove hope from your tongue, they are only you
    what could you be thinking?

Night Visitors Made Flesh,
In The Vessel of Your Creativity

(Inspired by Stephania Ebony / for Denise Dumars)

Night desire made tame
in the grasp of your vision,
    what time can not remember
    will be etched in eternal brain waves
    electronic memory, in the open mouths
    of those who dare to ask.

After the Fire

I lie in the ashes
    desire, memories, hope, love–gone
reduced to a same grayness
    except for the hint of shape
the sense of what was.

How to rebuild
    from such fragile dust
What brick can be formed
    with these emptied hands?

I gather what
    the wind does not take
mix with tears, draw a capricious design
    on ground willing to take
my final offering.

Standing on sooted bare feet
    waiting for the cleansing of the next life
dressed in ashes
    I spread my arms.

Bleeding Cold

The future taunts me
   the present stings
   a million shards
a mirror reflecting backwards
   inside out.

My heart hungry for you
   days when we were
   not bleeding alone
where we were not
   empty inside.

Breathing cold
   life taunts me
   days to come
no way out
   of this freeze without you.

The Taunt

(for Sara)

In the light of my smile
    you think stars and moons are born
not knowing instead
    I consumed their light
purple, blue and green
    so you would call me "Sara"
mistaking me for a perfect hug
    relax into my body like water
become my dog, spoiled and sweet
    let the night in my eyes
sneak into everything you believe
    so I can be your sexy reality
save you from all the curved somethings
    that pull out of the surface of everything.

Tomorrow, I will be "Jennifer" for you
    and in the large moving clouds
you will be 'husband'
    together we will see
twisting days and nights below us,
    all will feed on the shadow of our desire,
when they think only dreams have come to them
    we will slide into a moment of 'can not'
become the flames they fear
    the very dark they will not follow.

Forever, is the meal
    a deliverance of yesterday, the drink
the 'where' of my birth, smooth gravy
    to upset all that will un-become
in the breath of our love.

Fleeting Light

I wake in your arms
the most safe place I know
   wondering what is real, what is dream
the taste of death's longing bitter
   in my open mouth.

You turn away from me
still sleeping, the curve
   of your shoulder, neck and head
familiar landscape, I reach
   but don't touch your sweet skin.

I remember our last kiss, now
moaning inside at remnants of blurred dreams,
   not wanting to wake you,
there was so much darkness
   why can't I dream of life?

Tears on my face, I reach again for you
my hand frozen in sorrow
   what if this is also a dream
the darkness I cry for, your death or mine?
   my heart can take no more loss.

Death follows me, drawing shade
over the people in my life
   taking one then the other
leaving me dry of tears
   my memories thin and fractured.

Only you are left, lying so near
my arms ache for a last taste
   but I can hold you no longer
the others gone, I too must leave
   fading into the shade of rising sun.

They say ghosts can not cry
but one tear is left
   on the pillow we shared
the dark dream I must return to
   awaits my fading shade.

I'll Take My Truth on the Side

(For Tom)

I smile at the open wounds laid on fine china
    your words remind me
of all the bones rattling on the table,
    the foolish desire half-eaten
the dreams swallowed whole
    under the light of denial.

I will sit at the table and feast with you,
    choice slabs of her and him
wait dripping with gravy of irony.

Perhaps for dessert we can dissect
    the remaining days
find one tender hope to flambé
    a wispy moment to shred
over creamy sadness
    until we sit with our bellies full
of the pity and bitter shame
    we had hoped to forget.

Like Water for Chocolate
(For Fay)

Your love smooth and fluffy
wispy magic delivered by
the curve of your smile, arc
of your eyebrow,

like water for words
your tales of the city
giggle deep inside the grayest day
swirling justice, injustice
to a perfect blend,

like water for fire
your fierce devotion protects
soothes, makes the way clear,
cleansing doubt and fear,

like water for air
filled with sweet scents
as you mix, beat, fold and stir
chocolate, butter, sugar,
love into greased, floured pans
all reasons to smile.

Like water
like chocolate
the magic of your caring
in our lives
remains forever
smooth
and
fierce.

Between

He leans into her dark dreams
   desire clear and yet, the edges blur,
she breathes in his fear and wonders
   what else lies between unfilled cracks
widening like his smile.

She leans into the bright air
   between them and breathes in his desire,
clear and shiny, fear and hope,
   snowflakes caught in between
words unspoken, like the breath
   between his smile.

He learns to listen and *can* not stand
   the howling madness in her eyes,
still he leans into her dreams
   listening for his name, hoping her
whispers will contain his desire
   but can *not* stand the screaming truth
falling around him,
   delicate snowflakes
      on a sunny day.

Earth's Blood

Black oil
  undoing life, feeding machines
how long it took to create
  how quickly consumed.

After the Tsunami

Waiting at the edge of the water
    for my child to return
stolen by the sea in a wall of water
    my tears join earth's blood
the surge back and forth, water
    filled with the debris
of human folly, buildings wiped
    clean from islands, reconstructed
land, swept clear of sticks and bricks.

Waiting at the end of the world
    for my baby to return
stolen from my arms as I ran,
    not fast enough, from
Earth's angry swell, one exhalation
    miles away and my womb cries
my tears join the waves slapping
    my chest, my throat raw
pleading for my child.

Waiting at the end of my mind
    for my life to return
each body that floats by
    fills me with hope, but still
no sign of my sweet baby
    his brown eyes smiling
his joyful laugh, plump arms open
    for me, legs springing as he
bounces on my lap.

I want to go deep into the swelling water
    find my child, but I stay on
the beach, waiting for the sea to return
    him to me, afraid to leave
I hear his cry in my heart, I can not
    leave him alone, I will not go
even as the sand shifts under me
    I wait unable to move
dreams of my baby wait between my breath.

Madness Has Wings

Like uncontrollable laughter,
    my dreams gather in tight binding around my eyes,
    thirsting for a tall dark sip of rain I tear lines
    in the memories dancing on my arms.

Little black and white images of us together
    appear in sidewalk cracks, I try not to stare
    wishing it would rain, wishing the ants would stop
    laughing, there is no place for tiny thoughts to hide.

They want to give me colorful pills, take this, take that
    as if a whole pharmacy could put me back together again,
    the cracks in my smile are just the beginning, I thirst
    for rain, for ants, for anything that won't laugh.

Sizzling fills my ears, my mind is on fire, again
    smokeless and efficient, reason burns away,
    where are my clothes, my dreams, my love
    how did I get here, on the sidewalk—try not to stare.

Like inconceivable inventions, my madness has wings
    leaving me to bind my ears so my brain won't fall out
    it takes all the colorful pills to stop the rain from laughing,
    even my own hands stare at my failure to connect.

Little moments pass before I realize that mathematics is all lies
    there is no gravity, or hunger, they tell us what to feel, to think
    leaving no space for the truth, I release my hold, no longer willing
    to play, finally floating away from the stares and laughter.

The Barn

It stands alone
  gray wood stripped of paint
doors long gone,

the sunlight stabs
  through its broken roof
the inner darkness splits into jagged shadows,

abandoned, waiting to be torn down
  no one will reenter here
memories of life long gone.

My womb moans with the ghost
  of the broken structure
both emptied, we wait to be torn down.

Dreams of the Night Bird

Inside
    the Shadow Bird
spreads wings edged in
    stainless steel
shrieks through new-born nightmares
    grins with half-closed eyes
at a world ripe for its hungry grip.

At night
    it pulls itself from sleeping mouths
to drip twisted visions, shredded hope
    in unexplainable designs
on moon-lit floors.

It travels in the dark corners
    of tall buildings, grim bedrooms
beckoning with a hollow song
    to the broken, the forgotten
promising to devour their bruised lives
    granting one last illusion
the echo of fragile desire fulfilled.

A Failure of Neurons

Remembering nothing of the past
   I love you
my memory evaporating,
you take me strange places
buy me things that belong to someone else.

I pretend to know you
   my heart won't let me turn away
you laugh and kiss me
I like how you taste.

Tell me your secrets
   they are safe with me.

I paint a question mark on my forehead
   to warn others,
do not trust
   words falling from my mouth
my mind does not remember
what I say.

I smile at everyone
   safety does not exist
I don't know why there are
   tears on my face,
who am I
   a dog,
   a bird?

Other Bitter Memories

Like something broken and old inside
   there is no traveling away from the pain,
   old shadows slip between past and future
   stirring up the present, making little things big
   happy things sad, colors shift around the edges.

Gathering more light, more breath outside,
   there is settling in the vibrating air
   new moments bloom between the pain,
   shaking down the past, making hard things into dust
   sharp into soft, colors shift around the edges.

Traveling away from time to the breath inside,
   strange colors stretch in the air
   cuts and scratches heal between thoughts,
   stirring up new moments, making light inevitable,
   time worthless, colors shift around the edges,

   other bitter memories fade.

Mistaken Identity

Wrong
    to think we are enlightened,
    to think we value life
        no matter how much money,
           what shade the skin,
           how big the house,
           what model the car,
    how shiny the bling.

It is only 2005 years a.d.
    barely a breath away from
        when we pulled ourselves
        from thick gritty mud
        evolved upright,
    barely a blink from
        when we traveled the land,
        searching for food,
        leaving behind the weak, old, sick.

Mistaken to believe
    we understand the
        magnificence of new life,
preciousness of our elderly.

It is a good sleight of hand
    we perpetrate on ourselves,
    to think that we care.

We are mistaken.

poem #3

ramble on, enchanted dark thing
for only the Unaware dare see us
stumble on, skeptic deadling
our words remain uttered thus
providing the Shadowed king
mordacious subjects to discuss.

Mermaid in the Bronx

Walking along Kingsbridge Road to the bus stop
    she wondered at the shadowed life dragging behind,
      even the roar of cars and buses couldn't hide the soft murmur
    of ocean waves calling, her feet bled in shoes that never fit,
even when he took her to the best shoe-makers.

Sitting on the express bus to Manhattan
    she hungered to be surrounded by smooth, fresh water
    even though the lungs she now used would disagree,
    eyes closed, the motion of wheels against road
    reminded her of floating after a strong tail kick, if only she
could remember the words to free her of this unreality.

Designing clothes in an office on 36th street
    she drifted into smooth swirling lines, sharp fin-like spikes
    always wanting colors to be blue, green, pink, purple
    touched with sparkles of light, others laughed at her consistency
    even when it always sold, whispering to hidden memories of
first waters that all humans carry deep inside.

Leaving work early she takes the subway to the tip of the island
    sits in the park watching the river waves roll out to the ocean,
    she wants to dive in, go back to her first home
    will the memories return like dreams, her tail, her gills?
Or will she drown as the doctors have warned her?

Stepping to the iron fence she stares into the gray water
    wondering of the wet dreams, the man and his love,
    even the pills can not hide the wet, green world
    shimmering in her sleep, standing at the edge, eyes closed
how easy to let go, return to the quiet water.

Home is where the heart is,
    her heart lost, she floats unanchored
    tired of the words, the pills, hungry for the
    peace of water, when would she have the courage
to return home?

Clear Like Glass

She filled her mouth
    with the shadows of his words,
unwilling to be a victim
    any longer,
wounds meant nothing,
    pain, burning and sharp
meant nothing
    hunger, day and night
meant nothing,
    all became shards
in her heart.

The twisting memory of his leaving
    came through her eyes,
her voice,
    bloody footprints would mark
her coming and going,
    her life would become
vengeance,
    the weapon,
the meat of her body.

Living Between the Blows

Untying knots between breaths
    this life flows, closed eyes, lips tight
    where was the key when needed,
    a sharp thought could do the trick.

Waiting between thoughts
    box open, above blue sky
    inside fear space pushes against tight throat
    where is the horizon when the sky is falling.

Back against the wall, knots quiet
    crazy thoughts tighten around closed eyes,
    where did all the rocks come from
    throw without care, bones break easily.

Clipping wings takes a long time
    muscles tighten around sharp breaths
    inside magic is gone, no dreams vibrate
    loss, gain flip over and over and over again.

Sometimes living between the blows is easy
    sometimes it takes forever for the next to come.

The Last Moon Rise

New moon sings
   a symphony of tears
   corners no longer straight
   all humans look up, the World changes
   one last time, nothing is the same.

New moon sleeps
   a breath of fire
   light no longer illuminates
   all cry in their beds, the Night dreams
   one last time, no one is the same.

New moon weeps
   a tsunami of desire
   time no longer has meaning
   all try to pray, the World lets go
   one last time, everything changes.

Openings

I left the top button
   Of my mind open, searching the wind
For the shape of time
   Instead I got
Smelly old fish and broken plates.

I left the top button
   Of my heart open, rattling broken windows
For a caress of emptiness
   Instead I got
Crumbly clichés and too tight shoes.

I left the top button
   Of my soul open, chewing slow memories
For the flavor of silence
   Instead I got
Razor-edged promises and no phone calls.

I left the top button
   Of my dreams open, stabbing old fears
For the sound of forgiveness
   Instead I got
A job.

All Hallows Eve

Let the wind blow and howl
   opening the door to sleeping souls,
in between life and death, like the last leaves
holding tight to a naked winter tree.

Let the wind blow and snap
   closing the gate to sane dreams,
we wake breathless and sad,
are we ghosts or do we live?

Clutching tightly to our blankets
   hoping the magic spell still works
our head covered,
our eyes closed tight.

Welcome the specters of past Halloweens
   watch impossible shadows dance
between the children trick-or-treating
on a moonless night.

Full of Tangled Remains

Twisting night dreams tear
   at my slumber, what could
   the rhythm beating against my back
   mean when tangled remains fill
   my mind, crushing all other thoughts.

These days march by in the way of all
   ignored small creatures, neglected
   time and space languish in deep shadows,
   recycled dharma lies quietly against my back,
   my mind, undone and waiting.

Waking brings little new, in one eye, reflections
   turn slowly, splashes of hunger churn in
   unpleasant corners of remote destinations,
   water, brown and thick, waits in my cupped hands,
   my mind crushes all names, dates, everything.

Sleeping brings me back to the tangle, back to the
   streaked bones hiding under muscle, skin,
   even stumbling in the dark to write the words
   does not release the spell, my mind
   waits for something between sleep and waking.

-299,792,458 m/s

In a vacuum, swiftness is important
   the speed of dark fundamental to
distance traveled from dream to loss.

Measuring desire fired at a great distance
   hunger reaches soulspace without lapse of time
even when need is fulfilled after a noticeable interval.

Dark can move faster than hope
   deduce nothing from this obscurity
Galileo was right, there is another way.

Place two ideas far away from each other
   with covered eyes, one releases held breath
the other inhales, both expire faster than sound.

In a vacuum dimming desire is important
   the speed of dark accurately measures
the lack of empathy available to a closed system.

Storm of Souls

the rain won't stop
   endless pounding
breaking down weak roofs
   crumbling concrete
opening the wound of earth
   slowly removing every path, every road

my ears hurt from the echoing
   the rain won't stop
my house is melting, brick like butter
   the rats laugh and wait
deep inside, the bones cry
   more water for the soup

the rain won't stop
   even when I repent
I promise in strips of skin
   in the blood of my unborn
but in this storm of souls
   there is no redemption.

fighting
smells like copper,
pennies on the eyes
of the dead.

Seeing the End

"Only the dead have seen the end of war."
—Plato

Only the dead have seen
   the end of war
their future undone by patterns
   blood-soaked in fields once green
the crop of bleached bones remain
   when the troops have left and weapons rusted,
silent witnesses to the shadow days of inhumanity,

shantih, shantih, shantih

No longer challenged to be courageous
   their spirits linger in still air, hands
over ears, drowning out the echoes
   of their own moans, eyes closed tight
avoiding images of new battles waiting
   to begin as the hearts of humans
close to their shared connection,

shantih, shantih, shantih

When did the first human command one to
   strike down another, how did the first blow
begin, breaking the bond to life, bringing
   the end of synchronization, where did the first
ghostly spirit rise from cooling body
   to finally see the end?

shantih, shantih, shantih

Mad tyrants draw battle plans in the blood
   of their children, generations disappear
as if violence could give birth to peace,
   the map of the world, borders lined in
broken bones, freedom drown in blood,
   the spirit of humanity hungry to live
even in the shadow of such death.

shantih, shantih, shantih

Burning

I want nothing
    my dreams burn in the shadow of desire,
    eating nothing they linger to touch
    some small part of my day,
    sweeping the vessel clear
    vines grow in tight patterns on the walls I have built,
    protection seemed so important yesterday,
    today I see the writing,
        warnings portending of things to come.

Wanting nothing my dreams
    sweep my life clear of tight desire,
    eaten by lingering parts of the day,
    yesterday seemed so important,
    yet I see warnings of things small and large,
        some touch the vessel of my breath.

Nothing wants to linger in the shadows of my life,
    even dreams sweep clear parts of the day,
    important warnings grow in tight patterns
    on the protective walls of my heart,
    I can not breathe in the light burning away words,
        still I see small parts of life cling relentlessly.

My dreams
    linger in the walls built to shadow my life,
    even I see them cling to the breath frozen in tight vessels
    sweeping the day into night,
    miracles wait in ever growing circles,
    the rain freezes above,
    jealous of the light
        pooling in small and large things around me.

I was deeply wounded once--
    grace heals.

ing

Burning in the Shadows,
While My Pen Softly Bleeds

(Inspired by Natasha Bennett)

Tracing moments of tears and laughter
the past is one dimension of now:
    the bright yellow sunflower reaches
    its center deep black, a universe beckons
    the tips of my fingers tingle
    the story begins.

Without

We breathe
    without knowledge
sleep
    without enlightenment
laugh
    without measuring
why not
    live
    without time?

Am Not

Returning from vacation
   to the rat race
I race
   but I am not
a rat.

Seeing war
   eat our young
I am angry
   but I am not
anger.

I am
   many things
and
   none of these things
or
   those things . . .

Who Am I?

am
I
you
love
peace
will
thought
anger
breath
silence
tears
song
dance
poetry
story
light
joy
sadness
all
you
I
am

Whale Riding

Riding the backs of
   dark, powerful dreams
the before-time singing
   in our skulls, ocean
waves under our feet.

This is the time to listen
   to the song of all souls
the moist tears of hope
   the laughter of the unborn
and ride the backs of the impossible.

Beautiful Meat

Transformation, returning,
   remembering inside
   layers of skin, bone, muscles
   without effort, light shines
   through star matter hidden
   deep within meat.

Relaxation, releasing,
   pouring over
   tickled ears, eyes, hands,
   without trying life dreams
   through moonlight unfolding
   deep within meat.

Imperfection, creating,
   memories, soft and broken,
   set in cells, DNA, genes,
   without awareness truth grows
   through double helix dancing
   deep within meat.

Dragon Love

Drawn by his fiery strength
  I ignore the smoke-filled air
my eyes locked to golden light
  in emerald-blue eyes.

Our souls were joined
  in one night's flight
my legs wrapped tightly
  around his long strong neck.

We eat outdoors
  meals cooked by his sweet breath
I wear a gown of discarded scales
  so we can lie together at night.

Ready

Stand ready to be
    amazing in this life
    magical and expansive
ready
    willing and dreaming
to be the big bang and all its cousins.

How delicious to be
    in this universe/galaxy
    swirling out and into
dreams forgotten by the sleepers.

Ready
    to become
    diamond fire,
untempered glass,
    cutting through
    slumbering non-believers
to bring life into
    newborn dreams.

Mythical Quantum Functionality

Elusive paradox, sub-atomic realms unfold
    below the surface, magically leaving walls and floors
undisturbed, in space there is no Up or Down, unlikely
    time and dimension keep reality at bay.

The uncertainty principle traces buildings and gardens
    for imagined beings to play in, subject and object
elude each other, working different schedules of existence
    the Newtonian world inverts and stumbles.

Spinning metaphors trick black holes and superstrings
    into enigmatic boxes, gifts for a new age,
outer space hides the parade of the Unexpected:
    red giants, white dwarfs, dark matter.

At the edge of All, vast Other Things recede,
    chasing the speed of light; science struggles to wake from
its own dream of measurable realms lit by chandeliers of photons
    plugged into archetypal outlets of mythos.

Yearning for eternal life, magical thinkers dream of science,
    science dreams of formulas and equations, symbols
painted on rock walls, language of the stars assimilated
    in flesh and bones, star matter untangles perception
allowing Being and Becoming into consensual reality.

A Dream

Come cry with me
    for the fleeting memories,
this dream, this one moment
in an infinite universe,

let our tears
    construct meta paths for dying stars
moaning in velvet reality, taking
one millennium to shed mortality.

Come live with me
    for this one infinite dream
this one dance
in a tear-filled moment,

let our dreams mean
    everything,
    nothing.

Spitting in the Eye of the Creator

We creatures of Earth,
    playing at the Edge of the Universe
we children of Adam and Eve,
    dancing on the tip of a pin
pushing aside angels and demons,
    bound by the concepts drawn on paper
we weave tight coils of manic theorems
    in hopes of explaining such madness
as bombs and guns and hunger,
    the knots seem apparent to children and cats
who stare in an attempt to understand
    the dizzying dance we perpetrate on a planet
who holds us in loving regard,
    even as we rip it apart.

The Shape of Words

Sewn in the loves
   pain
smiles
   joy of my soul,

booming in my ears
   sweet and sour on my tongue
sparkling shiny on the edge of my vision
   soft and rough on my fingertips,

dangling delicately from my eyes
   tied securely on my back
draped gently over my arms
   clasped tightly around my hips.

The Dark Dreamers

(for Necon Campers)

We dissect dreams,
    breathing and smiling on the edge of a thought,
tasting the flames of yesterdays in our open mouths,
    our blood carry unborn constructs rejected by reason
we open our eyes to visions running sharp in the shadows
    our lives, unlikely canvas for things: love, desire, pain, tears
opening, always opening veins to show the wonder, sweet and bitter
    the gentleness of determination
to tell a story.

Turning

Changing again
   not my mind to agree with
   a defined age group
   needs and thoughts
     controlled by commercial success

instead

   compelled by faithful moonlight
   to trade my unblemished skin
    for luxurious fur

Changing even though
   time between
   permits space
   to dream
    sleep
eat dinner by candlelight
   walk the street
   one well-heeled foot
   in front
    of the other

instead

   double over
   fire in my stomach
    heart exploding
   hot tears on my face
   boiling in my veins
    muscles split

NO

   still it comes

What is humanity
    if not the dominant species
    the ability to choose
    deliver power
        over animals

and yet

    curl on the ground
    larynx freezes
    screaming inside
        bones—

Becoming
    in spite of whispered prayers
    blessings under stained glass light
    holy water on fingertips

Redemption escapes me

    --bones shatter
    reshape
        marrow fills new form

Becoming
    while the scent of loved ones
    on shredded clothes
    impeccable manners
        fade with my steaming breath

again

    teeth become fangs
    tongue thick with humanity
    that tastes
        of prey

Turning

    spit a laugh
       through choked growls

Such thick fur would bring
  a good price
    if loosened from my writhing flesh

    anarchy loose in my brain
    howling at the moon
    my nemesis
      my love

Turning

    shredded reason
      raw meat
   driven away by the moon

need

to rip

warm flesh

hungry

hungry . . .

Point in Time

Starting at a point
    a mass of cells grows, expands,
blooms, knitting a catch-all
    to fall gently into, sleep for a while.

The point is a gateway,
    miracles entering this universe
dragging the big bang, reasons for
    love, life, hate, joy.

What is the point,
    a mass of cells, a net thrown
catching first breath, first heartbeat,
    places for miracles to enter.

A being grows, lives, withers, dies,
    falls gently back.

Dream Potions

Sleeping among the haunted mass of yesterday
   rank with the scent of the undelivered
I dream of potions to heal melancholy
   a way to unweave dusty disappointment,
forgotten dreams lying flat in shadowed corners
   gather shallow breath into a soup
of new beginnings.

Walking through unbreakable webs of tomorrow
   sour with the taste of neglect
I dream of potions to hide desire
   a way to invert hidden anger
left to eat away the mind, to defeat memories
   of inventive designs dripped into
the future.

Being empty among heroic concepts
   expansive with the caress of music
I manifest potions to focus existence,
   a way to travel without moving,
release thoughts tied to frozen convictions
   of becoming tree, air, child,
transforming complacent devotion.

Lying among the shattered thoughts
   wet with the motion of uncaring
I become potions of electronic growth
   a way to repair broken galaxies
waiting patiently to be heard,
   to open stars, nebulae, hearts
to the possibility of immortality.

Sweet with newborn desire
   dream potions of remarkable light
present themselves to my open hands
   the way to bridge the Infinite
become impossible paths
   to dark matter
made visible in a smile.

This Journey on One Breath
(for Larry P.)

born, live and breathe
one last time on this planet
love, laugh, smile and cry
on this planet, and touch
so many others – how wonderful!

Bell Rock,
Sedona, Arizona

Little Brother, why not weep
   remember the birth of the Last Dream
its sweet, soft edges shredded
   by pouring concrete.

Little Sister, why weep
   Eternity does not run
from your hungry arms,
   it is in your hands.

Little Brother, weep
   the hawk spirit waits for your tears
to cleanse the scorched earth,
   for your seed to bring life
to neglected dry land.

Little Sister, do not weep alone
   we are your ancestors to be
your alpha, your omega
   we hold you in our open wings
we will return the Mother to home,
   the Father to love.

Returning home,
   within our beating hearts
   the circle remains unbroken.

Holding You

Holding my breath,
   waiting for you to release
my heart locked in the moment
   your hunger held over me
lingering.

I know your secrets, the silent edges
   pressed in the shadows of your past
I lick your fingers, taste the tears
   in your endlessness
Shhhh—

Stripped down to skin and bones and despair
   you hold me, waiting
I can not eat, can not feel but for your
   touch, your raw grasping
reaching for an opening,

holding your life,
   waiting for you
release me
   let me breathe
this moment forever.

Cookin' Now

You bein' all smoke and nice
    And me all sweet and spice
They're all grab and run
    He's all lick and love
She's all peace and light
    Then it's greasy right.

The Last Dream

Tumbling, fast and wild,
   making primal shadows
   on the last soul, chasing music
   from still air, leaving trees and birds
   to wonder at the distant wind, so silent.

Slapping, hard and rapid,
   breaking concrete and cobblestone
   on the last street, returning to the earth
   what was taken, crumbs of blueprints
   leaving no signs of manufactured paths.

Dancing, slow and light,
   washing dust and soot from tall grass
   into patient soil, inside each tree branch
   rain cleanses the way for new visions,
   removing the need to count time.

The last dream wanders land lost and found,
   each step leaves a moist print of what used to be,
   without tears or laughter to sustain,
   the balance is relaxed, nothing left
   to feed on, the last dream is at last, no more.

Falling Away

Falling away from Earth
   releasing time and pain
an exhalation of demons
   wait to chew at bones left behind
finally between breaths
   reborn in no recognizable image
dreams tangle in the River of No-End
   dance on the thin edge of sanity,
precious memories of motion, small and slow.

Falling away from place and joy
   releasing Earth, demons wait
unable to exhale time or pain, finally between
   being and rebirth, between breath and no-breath
images dance in the River, thin and small
   precious motion, sweet memories
chew at bones left sleeping.

Falling away from demons who wait
   an exhalation of dreams chew at precious bones
left between Earth and the River,
   waiting to dance in the motion of memories,
finally able to release space and time and joy.

Falling, released from being, the River
   dances, between now and never
finally exhaling dreams, tangled and sweet.

Reborn, waiting between no more.

Dreaming the World

Dreaming the shared dream, we imagine
    each other walking on a planet,
    chaos added for mystery
    myth sprinkled over for sweet poetry
    gods and goddesses smiling at the play
    of humans, wisdom manipulated by infants.

Spinning the Universe, we imagine
    big bang, galaxies, solar systems
    expanding in a infinite mixing bowl
    out and in, wide open, densely closed
    pulse of a billion light-years, inharmonious
    meaningful patterns of fictionalized dreams.

Drumming the Cosmos, we imagine
    rhythms preparing our brains,
    menses, life, death, waxing moon
    patterns to make us listen, this story
    never-ending, when all goes cold,
    fading to black, the rhythm remains.

Dreaming the World in the World, we cry,
    what matter of myth have we spun
    in our shared madness, childish magic
    at play in the space of a wink, in between
    rhythms created to bring us to the ever
    unfolding Now, imagine infinite evolution.

Presence

Being Present
    as in: Be Here Now
clichéd
    yet strangely clear.

Being here
    as in there's no where
else to Be.

Try yesterday:
    being before, dusty and faded
what to do with the Past,
    except to remember it wrong,
change it into something better
    twist it into something worse
when all it is
      is gone.

Try tomorrow:
    being in the yet to come
translucent, ghostly
    some things that might be
some things to worry about, hope for
    filling the brain with what-ifs
distracting the soul from where
      it is.

Now:
    taste silky life
in the middle of a whisper,
    smile at the fullness of beauty
here is life
    fluttering and pulsing
even when broken or
    covered with mud.

Being Now
    infinite
    immortal
    enduring
      Grace.

Inevitable Singularity

Before
    a hand had five fingers, a body two arms,
    humans the capacity to love and hate, give and take,
    choice, a hidden agenda, created predictable consequences.

After
    spatial-temporal needs influence body development
    common sense comes in a bottle, clocks are meaningless,
    ripe for transformation, the universe continues to expand.

Before
    BLT was bacon, lettuce, tomato on whole-wheat or white
    Artificial Intelligence lived in the dreams of scientists and writers,
    a fork was a fork, a spoon—a spoon.

After
    nano-brain-computer interfacing creates food in the stomach,
    school children play with critical technologies at recess,
    trash becomes precious input to self-evolving systems.

Before
    becomes After
    when the Universe is rewound by the
    One Quantum Computer before it is turned on.

Rules

Invisible lines draw
   semi-reasonabilities,
   turn on carefully placed lights
   delivering new sameness,
   different, yet cloned from
   mis-shaped complications.

Compare insubstantial
   dark matter to
   irrational conclusions
   growing neglected
   responsibilities
   mis-understood platitudes.

Same-ness binds change
   in space and time
   shattered bags of past-present
   repopulate lists
   denied madness
   running wild in the blood.

One More Learning Distraction

Flesh body, another excursion into distraction
    on the road of enlightenment, pleasure and pain
as all things evolve, ending is inevitable, every star,
    every meat body will decay, how will we Be
in the ever evolving existence, infinity pulsing
    beneath each dream, when will we Be
in the comfort of academic equations,
    books, tests, outlines, where will we Be
immortality designed in our genes,
    galaxies, stars, planets, this planet, who will we Be
when the flesh fails, neurons, electrons, spinning
    a message, listen to the developing radiance,
be afraid no more.

Indestructible Reflections of the Dream Child

Tasting creation's sweet touch, life whispers inside,
   inception from Light, mixed with star dust,
self-evolved, even before first breath,
   when the Dreamer awakens, hungry to discover
the chosen universe, it is not the womb who chooses the Child.

Touching Light's hungry whispers, the Dreamer sleeps inside,
   no time or space disturbs the Plan nestled in structures
of flesh, connected to the infinite Child: desire, joy, sadness
   are shadow puppets for purposes of witnessing evolution,
not of skin or desire, the Child chooses a womb.

Hearing the wind moving across wild grass, the Child awakens,
   peels away the veil of Thought, pushes through,
mouth open, eyes closed, there is no doubt, the first Breath
   bittersweet, tasting the promise of large and small things to come,
of mirrored shapes carved from other stuff, the Dreamer chooses.

Speaking no sounds, hungry for desert and ocean, wind and rain
   the Child remembers purpose simple and clear, life
self-continuing and bright, a place to play,
   try not to harm, bow to Light,
unremember the Dream chosen.

Life reflected in growing eyes,
   small smiles recognize this is not
what has been, only reality refocused,
   choosing this life to unfold,
the Child tastes brilliant adventure ahead.

Perfection

In the middle of an idea
   no good
   no bad
   everything balanced
where it should be.

The coin does not flip
   light, dark, it
   expands in each molecule
   infinitely in the moment
of everything.

Beautiful, complete
   void of fear
   void of hope
   immortal light
forever . . .

Unfolding

Inside each heartbeat
    stones flatten, create corners
twisted by dark birth water.

Lines on the edge of the path
    follow crooked shapes
no one is the same as the next.

Open the outline inherited
    from guilt, reshape
into new growth.

Walk without doubt
    outside the lines
fingers dancing in cool air.

Turning, twisting, fingers crease
    flat into infinite dimensions
breaking all rules, undoing before.

Newly born, accepting new life
    Now never gives up,
new shapes carry everything.

Letting Go

Give away promise and desire,
    dreams and needs,
see yourself as you Are,
    expand,

Be the Now you search for,
    the Now that eludes forward
thinkers, dream only of Nothing,
    have Everything.

What if you are the Source,
    the genius, all purpose?

What could be sweeter than infinity,
    smoother than immortality.

Be the end of the story,
    where everyone lives happily ever after.

So mote it be.

Painting Chaos

(inspired by Dali)

Already in the premature
   ossification of time and soft
space, tension mounts, reality
   melts, corrupting
all desire and temptation.

Drawing a cube, the Dreamer removes
   its center, uses finger bones as knobs
creating the ultimate hope chest,
   a monument to Nothing.

Emerging from a metaphysical cube
   no amount of scented roses
cast out the humanity flowing through
   skin, even opposing points of view
does nothing, creating a hypercube within.

Approaching atomic physics, the ultimate poetry
   of de-construction filled eyes, perhaps pointing
to angelic purposes, even in avoidance of infinity,
   uncanny chaos mixed in paints capturing
each examination the Dreamer joins.

In that prime moment the slender hold
   on life melted into someone else.

Giving Birth

. . . to one's self, to process childhood wounds
    (no one gets away without)
born perfect, ruin begins with rules,
    parental weakness, societal concrete
structures, asphalt roads, the latest car.

The pain of my parent's parents
    is the first hurtle, a simple fact,
follow unconsciously a path, drift
    a little to the left, to the right
wanting the good mother, father.

Rebirth begins with stopping in the middle
    of the road, crying, raging at unseen
beings, unwilling to be angry at parents
    selfishly involved in their own pain,
dark rage signals beginning labor pains.

Blood in the veins rushes, what is the
    dark side saying to light, shadow self
the ultimate survivor doesn't feel pain or joy,
    only cries when the beatings exceed,
hides the light deep in a small box.

No longer a child, adulthood becomes
    a spiral of healing, be angry, reconceived
through doorways magical, the womb
    dissolves, return violence to the giver,
become your own mirror, reborn perfection.

Core Manifestations
(for Rick)

Going to the center, actions, emotions,
    thoughts dance, as is their true nature,
returning to the Authentic Self requires
    surrender, removing conventional windows,
opening infinite doors with invisible keys.

Lost in distractions, one path unveiled
    allows pain inside, ringing door bells
for entry to waiting bones and muscles,
    giving disregard free run,
wholeness becomes a distant memory.

Take pills, cut through skin and muscle,
    these paths do not find the missing light,
nor show the way from harmful patterns
    fashioned from the fabric of birth,
stop shaping new solutions to old problems.

Return to neutral, leaving pain in shapeless
    shadows, choose to be light, there are
new options to consider, places inside of present
    truth, without suppressing stress, let body/mind
speak, listen to disruptions manifest within.

Remember wholeness, ignore fragments,
    know life is light, brilliant and endless
in every cell, this body breaths magic, each inhalation
    a miracle, exhale unnecessary missteps,
there is no real pain in this one moment.

Balancing the core, let the sweet light enter,
    drop by radiant drop, until coherence flows
through muscles, bones, breath, thoughts,
    release past voices, future fears, pour
into the expanding center.

Belly Dancing

Gathering fire and wind
   earth and air
to spark along the edges of
   my hips, fingers, waist.

Rhythm tickles my earlobes,
   tendrils of movement
pull at my neck, shoulders
   the tips of my fingers.

My center, having carried life once
   fills with throbbing life again
finding itself in the strong beat
   the drum call to a body not young, not old.

Arms reach up, slow turning wrists,
   hands scoop and release air
balanced on one foot, ribs slide
   fire burns inside again.

Stomach slowly undulates, spine stretches
   a smile grows, even not young
my body repossesses fire and wind
   earth and air.

Say Love

You have captured my laughter in your sweet smile
    say saying you will stay
my soul rocks in your velvet brown eyes
    say saying you will love me
the light of your arms gather all my troubles
    say saying you will carry me
pain from my past healed in your love
    say saying we are forever.

Being Full of Light

Being a bubble,
    full of Life insubstantial
captured light dances, transforms
    becomes
    un-becomes
translucent walls.

Being fire,
    full of Light inconsistent
transforming matter, committing
    to become
    un-matter
echoing star dust.

Being water,
    full of purpose inconsolable
caressing all surfaces
    relentless
    un-doing
all obstacles.

Being earth,
    full and complete
giving all life a place
    continuous
    un-questioning
love without bounds.

About the Author

LINDA ADDISON is the first African-American recipient of the HWA Bram Stoker award. Her two previous collections, *Consumed, Reduced To Beautiful Grey Ashes* and *Animated Objects,* are available from Space & Time.

Her poetry and fiction can be found in the award-winning anthology *Dark Matter: A Century of Speculative Fiction from the African Diaspora* (Warner Aspect), *Dark Dreams* I and II (Kensington), *Dead Cat Traveling Circus of Wonders and Miracle Medicine Show* (Bedlam Press), *Dark Thirst* (Pocket Book), *Fantastic Stories, Hear Them Roar* (Wilder Press), *Dwarf Stars 2006* and *SpiderWords.com.*

Linda Addison lives in da Bronx with writer Gerard Houarner and an assortment of otherworldly items yet to be identified. Her life is blessed with an abundance of love and support from many friends and family.

This book shines with feedback from the writer's group, Circles In The Hair (CITH), Terry Bradshaw, Brian Addison, and Rick Barrett (who taught her the meaning of insubstantial and light).

Her poetry and stories have been listed on the Honorable Mention list for the annual Year's Best Fantasy and Horror and Year's Best Science-Fiction. She was Poet Guest of Honor at the World Horror Convention of 2005. She is a member of the Horror Writers Association (HWA), Science-Fiction and Fantasy Writers of America (SFWA), Science-Fiction Poetry Association (SFPA), and Black Americans In Publishing (BAIP).

Find Linda online at www.cith.org/linda and www.myspace.com/linda addison.

Back cover photo of the author is by Chris Lamb.

About the Artist

BRIAN JAMES ADDISON On weekdays Brian can be found hitting buttons under fluorescent lights as an IT consultant, a daytime activity that is correlated with graduating from Bronx Science High School and Carnegie Mellon University as an undergraduate. His free time is filled pursuing his passions of photography, tech and video game gadgetry playing, and listening to music of all varieties. On any given day he can be seen traveling around New York City with photo equipment he earned from working on an Nikon ad campaign in one hand, and a Japanese book in the other. Visit Brian's photo site: www.flickr.com/photos/badison to see what he does with the camera. And the book? Well, he may say that it's to stay current on what he learned in college, but surely it's in anticipation of returning to Japan, where Brian spent the summer at during a high school cultural exchange and has made a few return visits with friends over the years.

Books from Space and Time

The Steel Eye
BY CHET GOTTFRIED

In a world run by machines, being hard-boiled isn't enough—a detective has to be armor-plated! When a human client is blown to bits outside his office, the steel eye wheels into action that could earn him a one-way ticket to the slag-heap! The steel eye has locked gears in Isaac Asimov's Science Fiction Magazine, Pig Iron, and Space & Time.

> "Chet Gottfried's work is vivid, lucid and distinct"
> —James A. Cox, *The Midwest Book Review*

> "a beautifully crafted book . . . Sentence by sentence, the writing is beautiful, with its own singular quiet music."
> —*Home Planet News*

ISBN 0-917053-00-1 (paper) $5.95

The Spy Who Drank Blood
BY GORDON LINZNER

Ruthless, skilled—and expendable, because he's already dead! Tracking down the terrorist Free Thought Alliance seemed little challenge for his vampiric talents—but Blood didn't expect the mysterious shambler that stalked the Everglades!

> "Blood is a slyly humorous creation, the perfect hero for this droll, offbeat fantasy."
> —*Booklist*

> " . . . Blood is unique and interesting as a character and as an agent."
> —*Science Fiction Review*

ISBN 0-917053-01-X (paper) $5.95

Bringing Down the Moon: Fifteen Tales of Fantasy and Terror
EDITED BY JANI ANDERSON

This original collection finds horror in a Los Angeles barrio and a Georgia fairground; Nebraska skies and the New York subway; a South American dictatorship and a Turkish city under Mongol siege! Contributors include Elizabeth Massie, Bentley Little, Kevin J. Anderson, Lois Tilton, Gordon Linzner and others.

" . . . excellent!"—Jessica Amanda Salmonson

" . . . reminds me of the original anthologies August Derleth
used to edit and publish at Arkham House."
—Karl Edward Wagner

ISBN 0-917053-02-8 (paper) $7.95

ISBN 0-917053-03-6 (cloth) $15.95

Dead in the West
BY JOE R. LANSDALE

Death is common in the frontier town of Mud Creek, and usually final. After an Indian medicine man is lynched, however, bodies show up the likes of which Doc and Undertaker Mertz have never seen. Nor has Reverend Jebidiah Mercer, an itinerant gunslinging evangelist who challenges the demon behind the madness. Only by abandoning their hard-won homes can the townsfolk hope to survive a night of terror . . . but is it already too late?

" . . . Lansdale is to regional horror what Faulkner was
to broader regionalism . . . There are chills and chuckles
throughout this tightly structured novella."
—Mark Graham, *Rocky Mountain News*

ISBN 0-917053-04-4 (paper) $6.95

The Maze of Peril
BY JOHN ERIC HOLMES

To those who can survive, the maze offers fabulous mysteries and treasures from countless civilizations. When the Dagonites plot to keep these for themselves, Boinger the halfling and his companions must discover their stronghold, battle their warriors and wizards, rescue a friend, preserve Amazonia's waterways, and possibly save the world.
Inspired by "Dungeons & Dragons."

" . . . Clarity of thought and presentation, inherently interesting material, and a flair for the written word . . . a must acquisition for any serious student of contemporary creative fiction."
—*The Midwest Book Review*

ISBN 0-917053-05-2 (paper) $6.95

The Wall
BY ARDATH MAYHAR

Alice Critten comes to the Louisiana town of Bon Riviere to claim the legacy of her great-aunt Eleanor: a house cut off from its neighbors by a tall brick wall, with a jail cell lock on its single gate. Soon she is caught in a web of murder, abduction, and the supernatural; the doom that made Eleanor a recluse threatens Alice's existence, unless she can untangle the mystery.

" . . . cozy and entertaining . . ."—Al Sarrantonio, *Mystery Scene*
" . . . a beautiful horror-adventure book . . ."
—W. Paul Ganley, *Fantasy Mongers*

ISBN 0-917053-06-0 (paper) $6.95

Vanitas
BY JEFFREY FORD

Who was the mad inventor Scarfinati? Whence came his mysterious powers? What dark secret caused him to meddle in innocent lives? His bizarre life unfolds at the Carnival of the Dead, where a young woman seeks his spirit's forgiveness for accidentally killing him, and nothing is as it seems!

"Shades of Lovecraft and Bradbury make for an absorbing, fast-paced horror/sf/mystery . . ."—*The Bookwatch*

"Ford plays with words like a literary master, weaving his twisting tale gently in and out among his characters . . ."
—*Knoxville News-Sentinel*

ISBN 0-917053-07-9 (paper) $7.95

The Gift
BY SCOTT EDELMAN

Lovers Joey Amatio and Peter Grandin, reviled for homosexuality by the citizens of Allansville, revive the vampire that had terrorized the town generations earlier—and discover there are, indeed, fates worst than death. A 1990 Lambda Award nominee.

"If Rice's recent efforts have left you out in the cold, Mr. Edelman's book will surely light your fire . . . icy fingers will tap-dance on your spinal cord."
—*Mandate*

" . . . gripping, suspenseful reading . . . Edelman has added new twists and treated this very much as a story of people, and as such it works memorably."
—*Factsheet Five*

ISBN 0-917053-08-7 (paper) $7.95

Animated Objects
BY LINDA D. ADDISON

A first collection of poetry and prose, some original, some reprinted from such sources as Asimov's Science Fiction Magazine and Pirate Writings Magazine. Includes an introduction by Barry N. Malzberg and "Little Red in the Hood," on the Honorable Mention list in the Tenth Annual Year's Best Fantasy & Horror (1997).

> "Addison has enough invention for two writers.
> And enough heart for three."
> —Terry Bisson

ISBN 0-917053-09-5 (paper) $7.95

ISBN 0-917053-10-9 (cloth) $14.95

Going Postal
EDITED BY GERARD HOUARNER

Nineteen all new science fiction, fantasy and horror tales of madness and people who've been pushed too far, from amusement park employees to dumped lovers.

> "An anthology with but a single subject—yet a fascinating one. . . . Buy this book as a manual in modern survival training and as an assortment of Hitchcockian shivers."
> —Paul Di Filippo, *Asimov's Science Fiction Magazine*

> "The stories are much more varied than in most original anthologies: there are a lot of excellent ones . . . The quality level here is as high or higher than in most anthologies from major publishers."
> —*SF Chronicle*

ISBN 0-917053-11-7 (paper) $10.00

Dead Cat Bounce
BY GERARD HOUARNER (ILLUSTRATED BY GAK)

Follow the adventures of a deceased cat as it struggles to return to the land of the living. An illustrated fable to horrify the inner child. A 2001 Stoker Award nominee.

> "This poignant story manages to mix Don Marquis's Mehitabel with Karloff's Mummy in a charming creepy-funny fashion, a tone captured perfectly in numerous B&W drawings by a mysterious artist known only as GAK."
> —Paul Di Filippo, *Asimov's Science Fiction Magazine*

ISBN 0-917053-12-5 (paper) $5.00

Consumed, Reduced to Beautiful Grey Ashes
BY LINDA D. ADDISON

A collection of poetry to capture the path between things gone bad and transformation.

> " . . . reveals the little horrors of the days, the curiously individual science fictions of the nights, the fantasies where 'tomorrow will be reborn'."
> —Charlee Jacob

ISBN 0-917053-13-3 (paper) $7.00

The Mirror
BY NATALIA LINCOLN

A vampire glimpses his reflection in a mirror for the first time in eight hundred years . . . his victim, a young woman lost in the modern city, finds herself pulled into an ancient quest. Natalia Lincoln's epic tale of obsession, bloodlines, and an undying curse richly evokes medieval Eastern Europe and present-day New York.

> "A vivid dark world of punks, demons, and blood, of red velvet and black leather dusters. Driven by necessity, dread, and love, these characters carve their names on our hearts so we will never forget."
> —Jeanne Cavelos, editor, *The Many Faces Of Van Helsing*

ISBN 978-0-917053-15-3 (paper) $19.99

Order Form

Space & Time, 138 West 70th Street (4-B)
New York, NY 10023-4468

Please send me the titles checked below:

____ *The Steel Eye* by Chet Gottfried @ $5.95

____ *The Spy Who Drank Blood* by Gordon Linzner @ $5.95

Bringing down the Moon edited by Jani Anderson

____ @ $7.95 (paper)

____ @ $15.95 (cloth)

____ *Dead in the West* by Joe R. Lansdale @ $6.95

____ *The Maze Of Peril* by John Eric Holmes @ $6.95

____ *The Wall* by Ardath Mayhar @ $6.95

____ *Vanitas* by Jeffrey Ford @ $7.95

____ *The Gift* by Scott Edelman @$7.95

Animated Objects by Linda D. Addison

____ @ $7.95 (paper)

____ @ $14.95 (cloth)

____ *Going Postal* edited by Gerard Houarner @ $10.00

____ *Dead Cat Bounce* by Gerard Houarner @ $5.00

____ *Consumed, Reduced To Beautiful Grey Ashes* by Linda D. Addison
@$7.00

____ *The Mirror* by Natalia Lincoln @ $19.99

____ *Being Full of Light, Insubstantial* by Linda D. Addison @ $10.00

____ *Space And Time Magazine* (current issue) @$5.00

$_____ total of items

1.50 postage & handling

_____ sales tax (New York residents for book orders only)

_____ total enclosed (check or money order)

NAME _____

ADDRESS _____

_____

_____